Sibling Rivalry Press, LLC
13913 Magnolia Glen Drive
Alexander, AR 72002

ISBN: 978-0-9832931-6-3

First Sibling Rivalry Press Edition, September 2011

www.siblingrivalrypress.com

FAT GIRL

jessie carty

SiblingRivalryPress

www.siblingrivalrypress.com

To anyone who has ever looked at their reflection and thought: I'm just not good enough. But, especially, to my two sisters with whom I share DNA: Nina and Edna because they are nothing less than amazing.

Acknowledgements

"1990's Fat Girl" – *Southern Women's Review*
"All I Wanted Was a Donut" – *Poetry Hickory Anthology*
"Cracked" – *Hamilton Stone Review*
"Class Reunion" – *Diverse Voices Quarterly*
"Fat Girl at the Drug Store" – *Fag/Hag: A Scandalous Chapbook of Fabulously-Codependent Poetry* (Sibling Rivalry Press)
"Fat Girl at the YMCA Pool" – *The Dead Mule*
"Fat Girl on Fashion" – *Young American Poets*
"Fat Girl: The Superhero" – *Wild Goose Poetry Review*
"Fat Girl's Wedding Picture" – *The Hat*
"Goddess" – *ken*again*
"I'm Trying Weight Watchers" – *The Dead Mule*
"The Summer She Left" – *The Red Clay Review*
"Women of Willendoff: The Artifact" – *blue fifth review*

Contents

10   Woman of Willendoff: The Artifact
11   Basic Geometry
12   Thunder Thighs
14   Fat Girl: The Superhero
15   Fat Girl at the OB/GYN
16   The Summer She Left
17   The Artifact: Autopsy
18   Cracked
19   1990's Fat Girl
20   Fat Fingers
21   Waif
22   All I Wanted Was a Donut
23   Fat Girl on Fashion
24   La Grande Femme dans Chez Petite
25   Persephone
26   Goddess
27   Fat Girl Swimwear

28 The Fat Girl on Grooming
29 I Love My Biceps
30 I'm Trying Weight Watchers
31 Visual Therapy
32 Fat Girl's Wedding Picture
33 The Banquet
34 Fat Girl Snowed in on a Business Trip
35 The Greeter
36 Fat Girl on Air Travel
37 Fat Girl at the Drug Store
38 Class Reunion
39 I'm Baking Cookies
40 That Brownie Is Staring at Me
41 The Artifact: Last Meal
42 Super Supreme
43 And Then She Fell
44 Ill-Fitting
45 To the Fat Girl at the YMCA Pool

Woman of Willendoff: The Artifact

Nothing that is not there, and the nothing that is
Wallace Stevens – The Snow Man

The Venus of Willendoff, tinted in red was misnamed.
She predated Venus mythology by millennia.

Her pronounced belly, breasts and vulva suggest
something fertile yet how

could she hold up an infant? Her tiny arms - crossed
over her chest - have no palms. She

has no apparent face with which to watch a child.
Without feet she wouldn't run. She would

instead be present, provocative, always available
for procreation. Perhaps that's why

she had time to have plaits put in her hair. Braids
that remind me of the weaving of baskets

and I wonder what if I put you in basket, could I then
crack you, egg like for Easter to see

what is inside; what
you are and aren't.

Basic Geometry

As my sister asks me to watch her kids
while she goes into the public restroom,
I think of how un-private our lives are.

When my mother took us into restrooms,
I couldn't help wanting to look.
What was under her clothes?

I had seen under my shirts and shorts,
seen my square, flat shape
so different from the women

in the Penney's catalog with their
circles in the cups of their bras
and the dark triangles in their panties.

Mom wasn't like them either. She
was round. I wanted to find where her
edges were, where I might begin to curve.

Thunder Thighs

She's eight years old.
The Polaroid chops her off
above the eyebrows,
in the middle of the knee.

She could be partially
bald or a double
amputee for all anyone
would know but you

knew her before
she was in that photo
and what you call her
is Thunder Thighs

despite her average
face, thin torso, short
stature. Her hands
are behind her back,

the better to hide
them from their
accuser who will
assume they are

cookie crumb covered
or scratchy with
potato chip salt
instead of just sweaty

from pre-puberty
genetics already
showing in the girl
who eats radishes

and carrots raw
as snacks before
they are turned into
diet food and become

tasteless and unable
to clap her hunger.
You don't realize
she is more than cottage

cheese hips, more than
a cupcake face. She is
Athena, brave enough
to wear orange checked shorts.

Fat Girl: The Superhero

You won't be Wonder Woman
because you wouldn't wear
that outfit. Although, when
you were five, and not fat
you had those red boots
that you swore made you run faster.

Your least favorite is Super Girl,
the girl, the skirt, how close the word
Super is to Supper and how you'd fall
out of the sky targeting
the first red Wendy's sign.

Maybe you could be the awkward/
obscure Gigantic Girl whose gift
was growing tall, not out you notice,
but up. She was hefty, having
strength and size like a man.

Fat Girl at the OB/GYN

On the second day of my first period,
my mother took me to the doctor.

Thank God, I thought as another cramp
clutched my left side.

At 13, I was taller than the doctor
and wider than my mother

who was sure my puberty
was advancing like cancer.

Mom told the doctor I needed the pill.
She was sure my love

of Twinkies would translate
to my fat thighs opening at any touch.

The Summer She Left

There was   an empty crib

                     no bathing

a lack of gospel

        and plastic hangers

                          on the floor.

      So I made corn on the cob

                       for dinner

   covered in foil

   coated in butter

                     on a red grill.

                     There was no

                meat

          no greens

but   there was   water without ice

          and sweat

   weeping from a glass

                 forming a circle

   on the table

fat as the moon

at its fullest.

The Artifact: Autopsy

The first cut is known as the Y incision. Starting with the left shoulder, cut diagonally down to the right breast bone, repeat this like a mirror till there is a V above the breasts. Then cut a straight line across the wave of the torso, going maybe to the left around the navel until you reach to the pubic bone.

Move the V piece over the blank face and then grapple the lower part of the Y open with both hands. It will open like two heavy doors. The breasts, in this case, will not fit into the armpits.

Note that nothing escapes the opening. There is no steam. No mist. No fluid. It is emptier than expected, even as it is being full of one shape.

Cracked

I peel like a boiled egg.
First, I knock my head
to create a crack. Then,
I reach up to pull
down my left side. I'm
right handed. I come
apart in little plates
of shell. Inside,
I'm white and soft.
I have to dig into my hip,
the fattest part,
before I'm finally loose.

1990's Fat Girl

The worst year was the one
of stretch pants and oversized
T-shirts. The year her favorite
shirt was from a concert. She had
Bon Jovi sprawled across
her copious chest, the B
and the l merging into her armpits.
The words bowed like a rainbow
over the rise of her boobs, which
was only slightly behind the size
of her stomach which morphed
Jon's face and the waves
of his bad boy long hair.
Down below, her strange short,
spindly legs were wrapped
in clingy black pants
that were anchored to her instep
with a little strap. She was dressed
like everyone else,
but then again she wasn't.

Fat Fingers

In my lap I clasp my hands tight,
straining the white
gloves I borrowed
for today, the

Baccalaureate service for
the seniors, our
upperclassmen.
My duty, then

as a junior marshal, was to
line them, one - two.
I tried to hide
my gloves ripped side.

Waif

She walks like her shadow
with her feet attached to the floor.

She's no thicker, front to back,
than an average man's thigh.

Her eyes measure the length of her stride
searching for any previously un-noted girth.

From my seat, I see the tic - the jerk
of an arm - as I crunch a chip,

crisp and caloric.

All I Wanted Was a Donut

I drove through the Krispy Kreme drive-thru
but they had closed twenty minutes before.
What happened to *Hot Donuts Now* blinking 24/7?

Next stop - Dunkin Donuts.
I stumbled through an order, "One glazed,
One - do you have lemon filled?"

I ate the glazed first because what I wanted
was the lemon, but the lemon
was covered with white powder

which was unexpected. The powder
flaked onto my black shirt and the white
dust still won't come out of the floor mat.

Fat Girl on Fashion

I stick to pants, avoiding pleated fronts.
I require pockets - places to put my phone
and keys - because purses have straps
that are too short, that leave the zippers
to cut into my armpit or
if I go with a longer strap that drapes
across my chest, the mouth of the bag
chews at the bottom of my breast.

When I wear a skirt I have to make preparations.
First, the skirt has to cover the stomach.
Then, I powder up my thighs to reduce friction.
Now, they have invented a gel powder
that not only soothes the skin but it softens
the little tags of flesh that have extruded,
matching on each thigh, like doglegs.

La Grande Femme dans Chez Petite

In a three way mirror
I check my look. I tug
at the tank top hem,
but it rolls up, resting
on the shelf of my stomach.

Through the slatted half
door, the sales girl asks,
"Can I help you
with another size?"

"No, this is just right,
I'll take it."

At a three way stop
outside the mall, I look
both ways. No one is coming
so I squeeze
the bag of clothes
through the car window.

It plops onto a well manicured,
flowered median.

Persephone

Binging I can do
but not the purging
or at least not of food.

CD's, clothes or friends
as loose as change in a skirt
pocket, swatting a numb

spot onto my thigh, those
can be tossed but not
the pomegranate

because even as it tastes
almost over tart, near
painful to eat I keep

chewing hunks of pulp.
As juice stains my shirt,
I pop seed after seed

from their ventricular holds
with my thumb until only
choking stops me at six

seeds, at half my life
destined for the cycle of eating
past satiety and into agony

while the other half, seemingly
thin, is really the wraith of a fat girl,
straining against the false

slim form because I'm
still hungry. I'm only chained,
temporarily, by the act

of counting, measuring, planning
and walk, walk, walking away
from living here and now.

Goddess

This is my hand, palm down
on the side of the tub
where my fingers curl like vines.

This is my other hand
which I plant against the wall
as I push up from the water.

In the rush of my own rapids
are stories of floods, of
myself dunked down and raised.

On the mat I shiver as my hands -
wet and wrinkled -
feel the round of my stomach,

the heft of each breast.
I wrap myself in a blue,
over-sized towel.

Once I tried to worship
this shape, this
hourglass form

in the goddess tradition
with circles, with chanting,
with promises of power.

But what of the comfort
in a robe; in that bearded
face from paintings

where his palms press
together in front
of his male visage?

Fat Girl Swimwear

My mother taught me that fat women
went swimming. Maybe they didn't
buy bathing suits; maybe they wore
proper undergarments under tank tops
and cut off pants but even so they'd
go to the river and float so I wonder,

25 years later, whether the outfit
was a choice or if it was worn because
of a lack of plus sized swimwear

in the stores we had to choose from:
Family Dollar, Kmart. I wonder where

she even bought her wardrobe
of polyester stretchy waist band pants
and the smock like button up, big

pocketed, flowered shirts that I find hard
to describe in any minute detail. I do recall
how proud she was one day when she

playfully tried on her husband's jeans
shorts and found that she could button them.
She never complained or talked about

her weight. She never dieted but when
she finally lost some pounds before she knew
she was seriously ill, she welcomed her

smaller size
like any
other woman.

The Fat Girl on Grooming

From the medicine cabinet she pulls the nail clippers.
She sits on the toilet, reaching down to her left foot.
Her left breast swells up into her chin. Grabbing
the breast, she places it on the left side of her left knee.
With her chin on her knee she begins clipping. She
can even reach the right foot as long as she leaves
her right breast dangling between her legs.

I Love My Biceps

I first noticed them in college when I started working. As I was lifting a tray full of frozen dough, my pink work shirt rose up into my armpit and there they were - little mounds of muscle underneath my skin. I wanted to show them off to someone. To say, see, I'm not all smooth fat and stunted shape, I have form. I still flex them and marvel at how they can hold my body up, at least for a time, as I move in and out of plank position or bridge. They give me hope even as my triceps sag and jiggle. My body has become the body of my grade school art teacher's. The first fat woman I saw who could joke about her size. To tell a student to be quiet, she'd threaten to sit on them. As she wrote on the board, she'd talk in rhythm to the movement of her folds. But, I never wanted to be her, well, at least not her flesh. I would rather have taken her ability to sculpt, to take the cheapest clay and somehow form it into a bowl-like vessel.

I'm Trying Weight Watchers

again. This time, a meeting before lunch
so I'll go and not use the end of the day
as an excuse that - I'm tired - like I'm
tired of being fat, but not tired enough.

Next to me, a woman in a jeans
jumper talks about using all her points
to eat cheesecake and then eating nothing
else the rest of the day.

I can see her, in her car - a silver
mini-van - with one of those variety
wheels of cheesecake from Sam's Club
on her lap, a fork in her hand.

Visual Therapy

I try to measure my hunger
in color. I see it as red,
flaming like a balloon
bent and stretched
into a magician's
side act - a giraffe
perhaps - unraveling
and up into hot
air and we are far too close
to the flat ass
of the sun that tells me:
Get up, it is the breakfast
hour, eat, choose yogurt,
stay unsatisfied. I'll call you
at noon and we can gorge
on pizza, pork rinds, mini
Hershey's bars from your
secret stash. And then
it is gone, pin popped.
I close my eyes, trying to feel
okay with just the square
shape of fullness instead of
rounded pain of wanting
that pushes me past comfort,
into the pink air
of calm, numbed coma.

Fat Girl's Wedding Picture

Her dress is off-white. Her groom
poses next to her in his typical
black tuxedo.

The photographer angled her. She
holds her bouquet
of fake flowers

in front of her thigh. I like
her shoes, brown and of
a medium height.

The Banquet

In a seasoned chicken salad,
the home baked croutons chide
the chives. They are the third course.

First, we had halved baked potatoes
smothered in sour cream,
followed by snow pea soup.

After the third course, the flaming fajitas
are placed. Their sizzling juices
torching the tiniest of taste buds.

I gorge - thinking, wanting, needing -
the cold calm of cherry cheesecake.

It comes on a white plate, drizzled
with white chocolate and sporting a sprig
of mint like an Easter bonnet.

After the final course, I excuse myself
from coffee and instead take a few sips
of ipecac tea.

Fat Girl Snowed in on a Business Trip

Today my stomach is full of cheeseburger and fries
        Two orders of small fries
                for two different meals
But I crave chocolate

Earlier I had watched cars trying to drive up icy incline
        on a West Virginian street
                I was like a speedway spectator
wanting to see one of the cars slide backwards
but they each climbed
        turned right
                at the stop sign
and were gone between houses

I'm bored with sitting here
        craving chocolate
                but after two orders of fries
those two different meals

I shouldn't eat again
        I sip a Diet Coke
                wishing I was home
but there I'd be worrying
the same
        and craving the same
                chocolate

just without snow
and there'd be someone
        watching me

like Jiminy Cricket

The Greeter

She is always your first contact,
The Greeter. The "come sit with me
at lunch" "any questions" "Here's my

extension" Girl. You talk with her about
TV shows you wouldn't admit to anyone
else you watched. You eat together. You note
how diligently she walks laps around

the office and how she eats her salads,
dipping her fork in dressing.

Then your other co-workers invite you to lunch.
You begin taking coffee breaks with them.

You don't notice how she slows near your desk
but always keeps moving.

Fat Girl on Air Travel

You're a pro.

Your shoes are slip-ons
that you have already
slipped-off to hold.

Your backpack is full
but there's nothing
in your pockets.

You don't want to blip
the detector that sounds
like the children

who follow you with their
shit detectors; with their
antidotes of circle, circle

dot, dot. You just want to pass.

Fat Girl at the Drug Store

She puts a roll of Rolo's
in her shopping cart
then adds a Diet Coke

As she walks by the freezer section
she opens the door to consider
the Lean Cuisines

Near the register
she flips through the latest issue
of O magazine

trying to find
a particular price point
a number

which makes it okay
for a fat girl
to buy condoms

Class Reunion

So what if my stomach
is rounder than you remember
or that my hair is shorter?
I'm still me.

Don't act like I'm different,
that I'm not the same girl
that let you . . .

Don't look at me with that
face. You are no
more Helen than me.

I'm Baking Cookies

My left brain asks –
Aren't you on a diet?
My right brain replies –
I've been on a diet
since I first breathed air.

As they took me out
of our mother, I started
gasping, reaching
my tiny pink fists
to pull the air into my mouth

as if I could chew it with my gums.
Where were you?
Do you remember how
our teeth even came in early?

We couldn't breast feed.
I moved on to solids,
to rolling cookie dough
into balls while Mom
preheated the oven.

I'd lick my fingers
as I watched the stove, as I
bend over now to put in
a cookie heavy pan
while all you will do is mark time.

That Brownie Is Staring at Me

I have something in my pocket
that belongs in my face.
It is far too close at hand:
most convenient, most tempting.

I picture it heated in the microwave,
possibly topped with peanuts
and whipped cream. I bet
you have guessed it, I bet

you can see my smile but what
of the tears later? Can you guess
if you guess for a long, long
while at the hours I'll spend

thumbing through photographs
from when I was a size 16, aged
15, size child's 12, age 8 in a used
Girl Scout uniform that is too short?

Me, in a hand me down brown jumper
with my beanie-less head spinning
around to look in the mirror, to see:
the chocolate in my lip corners, un-lickable,

chocolate that will need water, fingers,
napkins. I have to open my eyes if I
want to clean her up; if I want to straighten
myself out. I focus on our brown hair

and brown eyes that still match. We
stare at each other and sing "Twist me
and turn me and show me an elf, I looked
in the water and saw" the ritual.

The Artifact: Last Meal

An investigation of the stomach is crucial. Pull your blade across the great curvature of the organ. In this case, we are trying other implements because the organ is more like stone, like pumice. What does that say of this artifact, this form? With a chisel we gain entry. The surface inside is like mesh, as if the gut had been a net for what all is here - dirt, seeds, petrified wood, a seemingly intact plum.

Super Supreme

It's not often that I eat pizza
since it isn't low-carb or lactose-free.
But today I ordered a personal sized
supreme pizza and there you were.

You were part of the sausage,
pepperoni, olives, green peppers
and onions. The salt. I've
never found you in any other pie,

in any of the ingredients
on their own, yet somehow -
in this particular mix -
there is the taste of 1985

and Pizza Inn.
We went out to eat as a family
despite the divorce. We laughed
and dared my father to drink

the red pepper flakes from the dispenser
which he did without any visible discomfort.
He gave us quarters for the juke box
which only played country songs.

I ate the whole damn pizza today
even after I was full. I ate the last
slice like I could eat into memory;
as if the crust were your puffy

wrist, the vegetables your
veins, the cheese your warm cheek.

And Then She Fell

not for the first time, but the first time
in a long time in public. She shouldn't
be ashamed. It is amazing that more
humans don't fall as they, everyday,

defy gravity with each step without
even the aid of a tail for counterbalance.
And it isn't like she fell down from a
normal position. No she was trying to

do Balancing Half-Moon. She had her
left leg straight and had managed to lean
over to touch the floor with her left hand.
She had even formed the 90 degree angle

between her left and right legs but as she
went to make a straight line from that left
hand to her right up into the air-her body
thought better of such defiance. She

immediately declared I'm fine, I'm fine and
moved into child's pose where her head was
buried between her knees.

Ill-Fitting

This week she tries yoga.
A month before she gave up
carbs. You know this story.
You can picture her, if you
are polite, with a Raphael-like
frame. She had never tried
tortilla chips until she was
16. At 17 she always ate
a whole bag with salsa after
receiving her babysitting pay.
Back then, she also attempted
jogging. Next week, she'll
agree to buy XL Kung Fu
pants, so she can try a class.
And yet, they won't quite fit.

To the Fat Girl at the YMCA Pool

You think you have breasts
because you wear a padded
bathing suit; a woman's suit
with strategically placed
tropical flowers,

but your pre-puberty nipples
only stand up like diligent
erasers because of the fat
pressing beneath them,
not because they have
expectations of boys; of
babies; of want.

You lumber after your friends -
one in a Hello Kitty suit, the other
in a blue striped one piece with
white appliquéd flowers.

Out of the pool you pull -
pull on your jean shorts
over your wet, thick thighs.

I want to tell you my secrets:
to play small, to towel off
behind curtains, to ignore
the places you can't

quite reach.

ABOUT THE AUTHOR

Jessie Carty's poetry, fiction and non-fiction have appeared in publications such as *Iodine Poetry Journal, decomP,* and *Connotation Press.* Her first chapbook, *At the A & P Meridiem,* was released by Pudding House Publications in March 2009. Her second chapbook, *The Wait of Atom,* was released by Folded Word Press in November 2009. In March of 2010, Folded Word also released Jessie's first full length collection, *Paper House,* which was nominated for a SIBA award. Jessie has been a finalist in several poetry and chapbook contests, including placing third in the St. Louis Poetry Center's 2008 contest after which her poem "Sex Education" appeared in *MARGIE.* Her second place winning poem, "Inter-coastal," was published in the Charlotte Writer's Club 2009 Anthology *Journey Without.* Jessie works as a freelance editor and writer and teaches Writing and Literature courses at Rowan Cabarrus Community College. She lives in Charlotte, North Carolina.

www.jessiecarty.com

ABOUT THE PUBLISHER

The mission of Sibling Rivalry Press is to develop, publish, and promote outlaw artistic talent - those projects which inspire people to read, challenge, and ponder the complexities of life in dark rooms, under blankets by cell-phone illumination, in the backseats of cars, and on spring-day park benches next to people reading Plath and Atwood. We welcome manuscripts which push boundaries, sing sweetly, or inspire us to perform karaoke in drag. Not much makes us flinch.

For more information, visit us online.

www.siblingrivalrypress.com